Finding My Tail

Samantha Newbury

Indigo Dreams Publishing

First Edition: Finding My Tail
First published in Great Britain in 2013 by:
Indigo Dreams Publishing
132 Hinckley Road
Stoney Stanton
Leics
LE9 4LN

www.indigodreams.co.uk

ISBN 978-1-909357-27-3

British Library Cataloguing in Publication Data. A CIP record for this book can be obtained from the British Library.

Designed and typeset in Palatino Linotype by Indigo Dreams. Cover design by Ronnie Goodyer of Indigo Dreams based on original art by Samantha Newbury.

Printed and bound in Great Britain by Imprint Academic, Exeter.

Papers used by Indigo Dreams are recyclable products made from wood grown in sustainable forests following the guidance of the Forest Stewardship Council.

In memory of my grandparents,
whose love and wisdom I miss daily;

For my beloved 'Hubs' – home is,
and forever will be, within the circle of your arms.

For Theresa
with best wishes

Acknowledgements

I am very grateful to the Van Gogh Museum in Amsterdam for their permission to use the quote from Van Gogh's letter to Theo Van Gogh Tuesday 26 November, 1889 (Letter 823).

Being told I had breast cancer on 20th June 2011 wasn't a good moment, however we immediately found ourselves placed into the care of a very special team who, between them, have been there for us every step of the way: The L&D breast screening unit staff; Dr Simon Allen, Consultant Radiologist; Jan Chalkley, Macmillan Breast Cancer Nurse; Mr Michael Pittam, Consultant Surgeon; Di Reid & the pre-assessment team; The Nuclear Medicine, anaesthetic & recovery teams; HSSU, Cardiology, Radiography, Phlebotomy & Pharmacy; the nursing staff on L&D ward 20 & the porters; Jane Ford, Rita Patel & Michelle Thomas, Hospital at Home Team; Manta, Mildred & the rest of the outpatient clinic staff; Dr Mei-Lin Ah-See, Consultant Clinical Oncologist; Val Wortley, Vascular Access Team; Nicky, Sylvia, Sandra, Annie, Shirley, Flora, Lesley, Asher, Ruth, Rama & Jan, Chemo Unit; Julie, Penny, Brian & the other L&D Macmillan Volunteers; Chris Harris & the district nursing team; Lesley, Orthotics; Louise Rivett, Oncology Research Sister; the Mount Vernon LA9 radiotherapy team; Marie Browne, Macmillan Specialist Psychotherapist & Dr Anne Lee, Clinical Psychologist; Look Good, Feel Better; Kashmir Randhawa, Genetic Counsellor; Sheila Webb, Lymphoedema Nurse; Rebecca Ross, Complementary Therapist; Cherry Mackie & Pam Thorpe, Ear Acupuncture (Mount Vernon); The Lynda Jackson Macmillan Centre volunteers; and, finally, Dr Maria Stratford & Dr Aasim Siddique, GPs & the rest of the staff at Barton Hills Medical Group. 'Thank-you' isn't remotely adequate.

My thanks also go to family and friends for their on-going love, support and encouragement (and for hugs, soup, lifts, ironing, fluffy socks, flowers, daft phone calls, shopping and all the other many kindnesses that have got us through this past couple of years), and the TB 'family' for their advice, support and encouragement.

Publication acknowledgements

A number of these poems were first published in magazines or anthologies:

Bat, Christmas Wishes and *Something to Hang on Your Tree*, in Writing Magazine.

Watercolour, La Pâtisserie Automne, Finding My Tail, For Two Weeks Only, Gale, Siesta and *Storm in May* in The Dawntreader.

Encounter in the United Press anthology Still Life (2004).

For Sylvia at 17 in the Cruse Tyneside bereavement anthology Rowing Home (2008).

Where's the acid-free tissue paper? in the Baskalier Publishing anthology Extinction (2010).

'Creole' in the Bell Jar collection Bugged…Writings from overhearings (2010).

Day Trip in the Alfie Dog Fiction e-book One Word Anthology (2012).

lump in the Indigo Dreams Publishing/Macmillan Cancer Support anthology, Heart Shoots (2013).

CONTENTS

Finding My Tail

Finding My Tail

I am Capricorn.
A fish-tailed goat.
The Zodiac's ultimate contradiction.

My goat self, white furred
like the hoar-rimed Friday
upon which I was born,
with eyes the clear cold turquoise
of the solstice sky.
Seeking the austere authority
of mountain-tops.
Longing to look beyond the horizon,
the whole world laid out before me.
Yearning for approval and recognition,
but always just a little aloof,
for fear of falling.

But then there's my fish self,
my Mediterranean tail;
long and shimmer-scaled,
star-scattered with gold.
Warm and languorous,
at one with the world
and loving each detail.
Content just to be a part of everything.
It took me forty years to find it
and now I have, I am anchored
and can climb the highest peaks with ease
knowing I will not fall.

I am Capricorn,
a fish-tailed goat,
the Zodiac's ultimate combination.

Conversations with a Lesser Planet – Fugue – Part One

November twenty-sixth and it begins;
the music for our fifteen year pavane.
I sense a strange serenity within
as now, Pluto, you turn and take my hand.
Your touch is cool – behind your mask, your eyes
hold challenges I know I'll have to face;
you'll strip me of all vestige of disguise,
before you set me free from your embrace.
Your influence though, may not be denied,
whatever comes, I'll follow where you lead;
a wildness I've long hidden deep inside,
demands I seek adventure and succeed.
       Though we can't know just where this dance will end,
       already you're more lover than a friend.

Siesta

The day is a thousand shades of blue;
from horizon's palest opal,
to blue-black cypress,
and last night's stars dance
upon kingfisher ripples
in the gold-rimmed bay.
Hills and olive groves drowse
beneath an azure haze,
and turquoise waves whisper,
as they caress the shore,
'Hush, hush, be still'
and peace is a thousand shades of blue.

Full Moon, January 2006

The sky, as I walked home tonight,
was cobalt blue silk velvet,
caught in place
with tiny, faceted glass beads
sparkling against the fabric's sheen;
the moon, a huge,
softly shimmering,
Mother of Pearl button,
whose light topstitched
the stark branches of the winter wood
with glittering Lurex
and overlaid the corduroy fields
with silver gauze.

February Frost

Today has been rendered in chalks.
The colours are pale, powdered;
dusty pastels, smudged at the edges;
apricot, mint, rose, lavender;
a bowl of sugared almonds.

Stillness is essential;
the merest movement,
the slightest touch
and it will all dissolve
into the golden sunrise.

Even the breeze holds its breath.

Late Spring

March slinks in on silent,
snow leopard feet. Frost furred,
with claws of ice, it stalks the hills;
its spotted tail sweeping them
with fine, biting snow.
Puddle and pond alike,
are petrified, by the intensity
of its cold, blue stare.
The snarling chill of its breath
scours the fields, and the lambs
huddle close against their mothers;
their day will be a long time coming.

Respite

Now comes the thaw;
the steady drip and creep
of slipping blankets
that were laid deep
on roof and sill.

Icicles draw out like wax
and air that, yesterday,
scoured my cheeks,
now soothes my face
with warm caress.

And then the muted rush
of a branch shedding its load;
like some Deco socialite
carelessly dropping
her white fox stole.

Sleet

Almost,
but not quite, snow,
it splats wetly; vanquished
immediately by sneering
wipers.

First Snowdrop

See,
a single swordsman
has thrown down his gauntlet
to the frozen earth,
duelled,
and, with his fine green rapier,
won.

Now,
he rings a peal of silver bells
to call the others to arms
and they come;
advancing in ranks, battalions
and legions
of green.

Soon,
victorious,
they will hoist their colours,
gold, red, purple, blue,
to announce to the world
that winter has been conquered
by spring.

Clarity

Today is a day of pristine edges,
each leaf sharply defined;
each colour crystalline;
each image incised
upon my memory
like a paper-cut;
no room for fog
or indecision,
just perfect,
detailed
focus.

For Two Weeks Only

For fifty weeks a year they hunch,
a scraggy, grey, nondescript bunch
with scaly bark and khaki leaves;
unknown, un-noticed council trees.
But come the warmth of April days
there's suddenly a sequinned haze,
shimmering bronze as new leaves break
and sleeping showgirl dryads wake,
swapping their costumes, like the pro's
from those old Busby Berkeley shows,
to line the stage in vibrant pink;
glamorous, sexy, and I think
that someday, if they got the chance
to pull their roots right up and dance,
The Avenue would fairly beat
to their high kicking, tap-shoed feet.

Revue

There's a new show on The Avenue this spring
(the flowering crabs have exited stage right);
now silver birch are limbering in the wings
waiting for curtain raise on opening night.

They had a winter try-out with tableaux
to whet our appetites for what's to come;
in shimmering robes of hoarfrost, ice and snow
they held their poses spot-lit by sun.

And now they're dressing for the overture
in flowing ballet skirts of pale chartreuse;
the first act will be elegant, demure,
segueing into sultry summer blues.

The finale though will have a real pizazz;
quick-changing into gold fringed flappers' dress
they'll return as autumn's trumpets strike up jazz
and prove that they can Charleston with the best.

Bramingham Woods – May

The tide of spring has broken in the woods
and now the blackthorn drips with foaming spray.
Wide pools of bluebells lap the beeches' roots;

Legacy of the wave that's ebbed away.
The whisper of the new leaves in the breeze
reminds me of the quiet surf at play

And verdant scents, that tantalise and tease,
entreat like tiny ripples on the shore;
the wistful ache within my heart is eased

By diving in to wander and explore,
the limpid blue-green depths that lie within
whose dancing leaves and sunlight can restore,

Just as saltwater gently soothes the skin,
my weary soul that's winter-worn so thin.

Storm in May

The sky,
unable to decide
between smooth, blue satin
and white, broderie frills,
grows petulant,
hauls on a thick, grey hoodie,
grumbles, slams, bangs;
fills the air
with sulky electricity,
before bursting
into hot, angry tears.

Twenty minutes pass,
the sobbing ceases
and she opts for denim
with a full spectrum
chiffon scarf.

June

Now there is time in the evenings,
to kick off my shoes and walk
barefoot upon the grass,
and feel its cool, green livingness
beneath my toes.

Time, to smile at my flowers
and welcome the day's new openings,
and watch fat bees as they squeeze
into the spotted bells of foxgloves;
dusting their furry backs with gold.

Time, to run my hand up a stem of rosemary
and savour the pungent fragrance of remembrance.
Time to stroke the soft, grey ears of stachys
and listen to the swallows whistle
as they swoop high in the blue bowl of sky.

Time, to water my carrot and salad seedlings
and delight in the sparkling droplets
that bejewel the foliage.
Time to peer beneath the leaves of the plum tree
and gloat over the amethyst treasures growing there.

Time, later, to sit upon the bench, he and I,
and talk of little things,
whilst we watch the stars emerge
and the moths take wing
against the sapphire sky.

Bat

Where did you go?
I glimpsed you turning
tip-tilted on the edge
of twilight.
Felt, suede-soft
against my cheek,
the swiftest kiss
of wing-swirled air.

Then, in an instant,
you span upon
the delirious scent
of jasmine, shot up
into the deepening blue
and were gone – lost
in the sudden shimmer
of the first star.

Festival

Are the plums ripe today?
Nestled like shadows beneath the leaves;
their dusky skins, bloomed with white,
are taut about their golden, honeyed flesh,
and slender branches dip beneath their weight.

Yes! The plums are ripe today.
As my questing fingers reach to touch
a fruit drops, sun-warm, into my palm;
the essence of summer, created
by a small, fat bee with a ginger rump.

9th September 2008

The day they switched the Large Hadron Collider on.

It would have been disappointing
if the world had turned to goo
at eight-thirty on a Wednesday morning.
The doom-mongers predicted goo,
or all-consuming, miniature black holes
that would swallow up life as we knew it;
thereby scaring small children
(and not a few adults).

But the only black hole encountered
was the tunnel just north of Grantham
and I am glad that birches
are still shimmying in the breeze,
whilst sheep and rabbits graze
in peaceable companionship
and trains depart for Sleaford and Skegness
without the slightest hint
of gooiness.

Watercolour

Seurated with splashes,
Moneted with mist;
rain has rendered the world
Impressionist.

La Pâtisserie Automne

M'sieur Automne takes out his copper bowls
and marble slab and sets to work;
he tempers glossy, bitter chocolate
in which he dips the copper beeches.
Then mixes glazes, lime, apricot, cherry –
brushing them over sycamores and maples;
saving the deepest raspberry
for Virginia Creeper.

Filling his icing bags, he pipes
gleaming clusters of scarlet and gold
upon holly, rowan and cotoneaster;
and sometimes, overnight, he dusts
his wares with powdered peppermint,
draws feathered patterns in his glacé
and weaves sparkling webs of sugar, boiled
to three hundred and ten degrees.

Working fast to fill the shelves
he bakes a thousand different leaves:
curled chestnut brandy snaps,
pale poplar shortbreads and
dainty lemon, linden thins,
ginger-spiced oak lebkuchen,
brittle birch millefeuilles and
nutmeg speckled whitebeam tarts.

The ravenous wind and hungry frost
devour them all; until all that's left
are scattered crumbs upon the pavement
and the fruitcake scent of beech-mast.

Gale

Tumult whirling,
tumbling, whipping;
leaves go dancing,
polka skipping.

Rushing, grabbing,
hurling, breaking,
bins upended,
mischief-making.

Thunder rumbling,
fence-posts straining,
bursts of hori-
zontal raining.

Crashing, creaking,
key-holes whistling,
brollies turning,
skirts uplifting.

Sudden stillness,
blue sky showing.
Ray of sunshine,
rainbow glowing.

Haiku

Winter cabbages
in serried rows; the field wears
a bouclé jacket.

Going North After the Floods

It rained too much
and trees still wade
waist deep in water.

Fields dissolve at the edges,
or lie, corduroy striped
by sodden hay
and reflected sky.

Rivers swirl stodgily
like hot chocolate
from a cheap machine,
or have broken bounds completely;
re-drawing the map.

Late

Friday morning, running late,
missed the bus, so now I wait,
but today it's not a bore,
across the road the sycamores,
have been dip-dyed bronze and gold;
sunshine thaws November's cold.
Fallen leaves are whirled around
by a breeze that hugs the ground.
Seagulls soar against the blue,
of a sky that's made anew.
Everything is crystal clear,
it is no trouble waiting here.

Foxes courting, full moon

When we first looked
she lay at his feet
on the wet grass;
tantalising, teasing,
uttering the little cries
that had drawn us
to the window.

The car sent them running,
in opposite directions,
but, when it had gone,
he returned, coaxed her out;
nibbled at her ear,
nuzzled his way
down her neck.

She arched
into his caress;
darker than he,
her brush curled
around her feet;
their love
on tenterhooks.

Owl

Midnight.
The white ghost waits
on the moon-silvered post;
yellow eyes appraise me, and I
tremble.

Wheeeeee!

Do shooting stars squeal with delight
as they streak through the dark of the night?
I think that they probably do,
I mean, if you were them, wouldn't you?

Sunday Afternoon at the Park

On the lake
duck and drake
preen then flap
scattering droplets;
reflections ripple,
waver, glitter.

Tails waggle,
swiftly upended,
puggling beneath
a parasol of dock leaves;
green weed drips
from yellow beaks.

Shimmer of sunlight
on iridescent head;
long stretch of leg,
shuffling of feathers
then curl into netsuke;
one eye watching.

Where's the acid-free tissue paper?

Amidst the sparkling tinsel of the galaxy,
a small, blue-green bauble hangs.
An heirloom piece, millions of years in the making,
it has become a little tarnished,
this past two hundred.

It is a thing wrought of miracles,
from the microcosm of the ant,
to mountains five miles high.
Nowhere else are there snowflakes, Redwood trees
or a mouse that builds cairns of pebbles.

Glass fragile, still it hangs there, but,
too careless a flick of the fingers
will leave it shattered;
the fragments of its mirrored lining
reflecting the faces of its destroyers.

Encounter

As I walked up yonder hill,
through the glen
and further still,
I came upon a running brook
with water clear and,
in a shadowy nook,
sat a willowy girl,
with eyes like those
of the fear-filled deer.

When I looked again,
none but I was there.

Pebble

Half-heartedly, I tossed
a grey, and slightly dusty,
stone of an idea
into the mind-spring's waters
and it made a sound all its own.
Part 'splish', part 'glop';
throwing up some droplets
to grab the light and casting
ripples circling for thoughts;
plucking them, like daisies
to weave a chain of words
and when I picked it out again,
washed clean of dust, it shone;
a perfect poem glowing
in my palm.

Cold Fish Finger

There's a cold fish finger,
lurking,
on a dish,
in the kitchen.
I don't know
what it's thinking,
or what it's going to do,
but I wish
it wouldn't
lurk,
in that cold and fishy fashion,
when I'm sitting in the kitchen,
on my own.

The Hidden House

The hidden house at number sixty-three,
inserts a whispered question in my mind,
'If I dared venture in, what would I find?'

Secluded, dark, within its cloak of trees,
perhaps some long-forgotten magic binds
the hidden house, at number sixty-three.

What spirit waits within to be set free,
behind the shrubs and creepers so entwined?
I daren't go in – I don't know what I'd find,
in the hidden house at number sixty-three.

Niamh – Saturday, 11am

In the snow-lit room
the conversation moves, by turn,
from poetry, through memories
to the moon landings.

Whilst I, by turn, stare,
at the elephant on the gas fire,
the Simpsons poster on the ceiling,
or count the ribs
of the model skeleton.

And Niamh works, by turn,
upon my neck, my spine, my hip;
twisting, stretching,
moving me like a rag doll.
Occasionally singing
under her breath.

High Wire

The cornet sounds a shimmered fanfare
and a single spotlight paints a moon
upon the billowed, greying canvas,
lighting the little island floating there;
its lone inhabitant dizzyingly poised
in spangled amethyst and silver,
with tiny, heart-shaped sequins sewn,
by hand, upon her gauzy sleeves.
A pose, a pirouette and then
she slowly lifts her foot to take
that first step, knowing it will,
as ever, be finely balanced
between applause and ridicule.
Head haughtily high, she daren't look down
for fear she'll see
that all the seats
are empty.

100 Metres

The start,
the pump of heart;
the beat
of pounding feet;
the strain
to gain
the place,
the race,
to hear
the cheer,
to hold
the Gold.

lump

I object to your existence;
your, quite unnecessary, invasion
of my personal space.
I will not dignify you
with underlining or capitals.

You will not,
with your sneaky, snichty cells,
steal one more millimetre
than the thirteen
you have already stolen.

And don't even *think*
about a surreptitious diversion
into my lymph glands;
I guarantee, if you do,
you will be sorry.

I am serving you
with three weeks' notice
of eviction.
You will be, forcibly,
removed.

Make sure you pack
all your belongings;
there will be no
other possibilities
for you, here.

Chemo

We're temporarily hardwired;
cannulas, PICCs, Hickman's connected
to bags gently dripping
innocently clear toxicity
into our veins.

Outside the wind is slowly stripping
peach and lemon coloured leaves
that glow like lanterns
against a heavy sky,
which threatens rain.

Our lives on hold; we've learned to be
patient patients.
We bring diversions
that can be managed easily
one-handed.

Outside the traffic ebbs, and flows,
pausing only for the lights.
Birds alight, depart; the world
moves on, circling this timeless room
where, for now, we're stranded.

Sooner or Later

I'd like it to be later
so that there will be
more things to find; photos,
that include Auntie Sam,
in my niece's wedding album;
a handful of collections – titled to intrigue
more than a passing glance from browsers
on Charing Cross Road or ABE;
souvenirs from New York, Assisi
and other places, not yet travelled.

They will sort through old reels of Sylko,
a pair of pinking shears, Swiss army knife
and war issue mending kit that 'un-memoried'
will be just things to keep … or not.
They will keepsake things that resonate;
the purple flower necklace, the sparkly blue pen,
the brass and copper candlestick (silver-soldered),
the camera, the bowl of crystal eggs, pebbles.

I'm trying not to think of sooner;
that there may be insufficient days,
to publish more than one collection,
to use up the ink in the pen …
the thread on the reels …
to choose more pebbles on the beach
with my four year old niece,
to lie within the circle
of my beloved's arms
my head curled beneath his chin …

But … whenever
there will be no bones, nothing to indicate
that, in this upended summer, I had

a lump, a mastectomy, a pixie crop,
an Angostura-hued cocktail of exotic drugs.
No, just a water colour in the Book of Remembrance
of a small, chagrined dragon – captioned

'Samantha Newbury – Poet
1966 – ... whenever
(450 million years of evolution,
up in smoke ... whoops ...).'

Strictly Drip-stand

Dancing with a drip-stand, it 'aint easy,
its tubes and wires threaten to impede
attempts at forward motion; bloody-minded
it has five wheels so thinks that it should lead.

It helps a lot if you pick the right tune
for your vaguely ballroom progress to the loo,
something like a graceful waltz or foxtrot
(a Charleston, jive or quickstep just won't do).

There's just one more thing that you should remember,
to avoid an unexpected tango dip,
don't forget to take the damn thing's plug out
before you set off upon your trip!

The Partner

He does not idle well.
He huffs
and twitches, fiddles,
checks his phone;
resents this time
of enforced stillness.

He would,
probably,
pace if he could
and rail against
the necessity of waiting.

Instead he sighs,
sniffs, texts;
disturbs the peace
we've tried so hard
to find.

Pentameter

A poet may spend years trying to write
the perfect line of iambic poetry;
turns out my oncologist has the best
'As far as we can tell, you're cancer-free.'

Being

These past few months
I have learned
to be peaceable;
to savour the hours
when I must be still;

To take pleasure
in the lazy drift of clouds
through the spaces
between buildings;
to allow the ebb and flow
of other people's conversations
to rock me;

To watch, contentedly,
the slow traversal
of a shaft of sunlight
across the wall
outside the unit;

To let myself float
gently upon the ripples
and eddies of music;
to let the words come
in their own time;
to, simply, be.

Haiku

There is a rainbow
held in the heart's deepest core;
each man's hope of peace.

Home

Is within the circle of your arms,
with my head curled
beneath your chin;

Is the stone room,
lit by evening sun, that lies
somewhere deep behind my eyes;

Is beech woods, limpid green
in bluebell time
or deep with winter snow;

Is a thousand places
I have travelled
in favourite books;

Is high in mountains,
where gentians bloom
beneath a crystal sky;

Is sitting at the ocean's edge
with lace-edged wavelets
tugging at my toes;

Is within the circle of your arms,
with my head curled
beneath your chin.

To my Husband, Painting my Toenails

You make a better job of it than I;
all these years of plastic model kits
spread across the dining table
mean you don't overload the brush
or blob outside the edges.

Instead, with painstaking deliberation,
you dip the brush in Dusky Rose,
or Wild Lilac (depending on my mood)
and work from the middle out;
placing each stroke with care
to ensure an even coating.
Whilst I look at the top of your head,
hair close cropped to disguise its retreat,
and know that I adore you.

Thank-you

'I've bought you a present.' you say,
giving me a flat, crimson box,
that opens stiffly, with a satisfying snap,
to reveal, pillowed on white satin,
a new pen. 'It's a sparkly one,'
you explain, 'to write sparkly stories with.'
Slowly I slip it from its bed and it snuggles
into the curl of my fingers.
It is richly, September sky-ly blue,
mounted in steel polished like mirror glass,
and I can already feel its sparkle
nudging at my fingertips.

Touch Me

Touch me,
that's all you need do.
A butterfly brush
of fingertips
or lips
and you will strike sparks
of pure, wanton,
electricity.

Call me by my name;
a warm murmur
against my ear
and I am yours,
not just for this moment,
but forever.

Cup my head in your hand
and you may drink me
to my deepest depths
and I will be drowned
in ecstasy;
oblivious,
to everything
except the heat
of your palm
and the fusion
of our kiss.

Arthroscopy with Sub-acromial Decompression

You walk down at ten,
double-gowned for modesty.
So I negotiate the labyrinth
of pastel corridors
to find the relatives' room
and call your Mum;
then scavenge enough change
for a Wispa of comfort,
whilst the air-con flings shivers
at the windows – the blinds rattling
like instruments on a tray.

When I return your bed is gone
and, despite the drum of rain
underpinned with thunder,
the emptiness is far too silent
for my liking. The golf from Turnberry,
already mute, stutters;
the screen monitoring the storm,
whilst the wind exhales
in warm, moist breaths
and every minute counts itself
in heartbeats.

Worms

I walk around worms on the pavement
and let them glide wet on their way;
my great foot stepping upon them
would be a very bad start to their day.

Eagle

His is the Sierra sky;
the air, his element,
I will not jess him.
Give him his wings,
let him soar, high
in the sun-burnished,
upturned bowl of blue
above the desert.
He will not hurt the clouds,
they, and the wind,
are his companions.
I will wait, here, below
and feel the faint breath
of his wings upon my face.
He will return,
when he is ready, but now
he needs the sky.

Let him fly.

Wishing

We fling the window wide
and, leaning on the sill together, search
amongst midnight's menagerie
for the falling stars of Perseus.
Strange, how I feel closest to you
when we are stargazing;
the brush of your arm
against my shoulder
leaves its own
trail of fire.

What shall I wear today?

Fling wide my wardrobe doors and you can't miss
the veritable rainbow hanging there.
From poppy red right through to amethyst;
the jewel bright colours I so love to wear.

I've no desire for navy, beige or grey;
life's far too short to wear such sombre hues.
Presented with a dismal autumn day,
I'll retaliate with scarlet skirt and shoes.

In lapis blue I'm confident, serene;
turquoise empowers – bringing clarity.
Deep cyclamen's amazing with sea green
and silver lends a touch of mystery.

For summer days there's cornflower or rose
and striking floral prints of every kind.
Rich tweeds and velvets come out when it snows;
cold mornings warmed by crimson, plum or wine.

And even black's more fun than you might think,
accessorized with vivid fuchsia pink!

Embroidered

Aeroplanes, as small as needle eyes,
couch the sky with contrails;
neat, twin-stitched, machine run lines
that soften slowly into knotted stem stitch,
unravel into frayed floss, then disappear,
like spider silk, leaving nothing,
not even a faint chalk line,
to show that they have been.

'Creole'

He said it was,
when the old man getting off the bus
asked what language he was speaking,
'It's a broken French.' And he resumed
his one-sided conversation.

My mind had already registered
the 'Frenchness' and had delved
amongst its archives
to dust off snatches learned
more than quarter of a century ago;
creating dots of meaning
that somehow wouldn't *quite*
join into understanding.

Not French then, but Creole.
That explained the exotic twist
to the familiar, the dancing rhythm,
and, perhaps, the fact
that he said 'Yes' so much.

Thwarted

Someone on the bus
is playing techno-rap;
battering my thoughts
and stifling the poem
I should have written.

Small Things

Peace gently wrapped itself about me,
muting the engine's diesel rumble
and the staccato chatter
of teens on mobiles;
It flowed, burbling like a cool stream
on a golden summer's day,
and let my heart and mind be still.

Held apart,
I could see the little things:
a dandelion clock upon the verge
releasing its flotilla of gauzy parasols
to count the hour;
droplets scattering from the iridescent
green of a mallard's head as it bobbed up
from the rippling mirror of the lake;
the slick, dark, curl of hair
against the nape of the boy in front;
and the never-ending,
always-changing dance
of leaves.

Day Trip

When I feel like an adventure
no excitement can compete
with the rolling, swaying rhythm
and the 'trick-track, trick-track' beat
of the nine-eighteen to London
when I'm travelling off-peak.

I've opened all the windows wide
against the sudden summer heat,
watching the dusty hedges fly
and the dazzling fields of wheat;
relaxed and 'day-off' happy
in my dark blue velour seat.

I can study people's gardens
for ideas I could repeat;
marvel the funky artistry
of graffiti-clad concrete;
then we're in and out of tunnels
where tracks diverge and meet.

Past Cricklewood and Kentish Town
and the backs of terraced streets,
and Betjeman, at journey's end,
this aspiring poet greets
beneath St Pancras's arches;
the gateway to London's treats.

A Dozen Cranes

Long legged
against the morning sky
they dance their way
to and fro.
Taking
exaggerated steps
they twist and turn;
stretching, crouching,
carefully placing
their iron twigs –
building new nests
for London.

Synthetics

Until the favourites fall,
and fall they will,
from grace, from favour,
from their exalted heights of fame
to become old, infirm, afraid,
as must we all,
the fabric of their Lurex lives
will lie, patchwork-pieced,
upon the newsstand wall,
with Velcro headlines
crafted to enthral the rest of us
whose felted lives are lacking glitter.

A shame that we forget
silk and cotton wear better,
in the long run,
after all.

The Cape – 7th October 2006

Suddenly Lilliputian, I can't step back enough
to frame the immensity of this place;
the boundaries have been pushed so far
that there are no edges and everything,
even the dream, is built on a prodigious scale.

I've peered up the gleaming, blue-sky reaching stems
of rockets in their garden and craned my neck
to see the eagles' shadows, small as thunder flies,
against the dazzling, white-gold face
of the biggest sugar cube on Earth.

In our toy bus we've toured a giants' playground
of Meccano-gantried launch pads
and marvelled the huge Crawlers which,
antithesis of Dinky, take days to inch
their towering loads along pale gravel highways.

I've watched the green clock counting down,
felt the gut-shaking roar of unleashed engines;
taken an hour to walk along the Saturn V
reading the stories, that are now legend,
of the men who took that giant leap.

I'm overawed – it's all too big, too huge
to comprehend. They say, when it happened,
it stopped the planet in its tracks;
I was just a toddler – so why does all this mean
so *very* much to me?

The answer's here, in this, small, Perspex case;
the distillate of this vast history is tiny – a scant square inch,
yet strong enough to choke my throat and prick my eyes;
for here, beneath my trembling fingertips,
the Moon is, for a moment, mine.

Rose Cottage, Newton St Loe, July 1969

The music always takes me back;
that almost discordant flare
of brass and timpani – and I am there –
in a room that smells of ancient stone
with the very faintest hint of damp.

And I can see, from where I sit,
on the floor behind Granddad's chair,
grainy pictures on the screen
of men in funny suits, who bounce
across a pale grey landscape.

Outside the brilliant sunshine lights
the border to a blaze of colour
and, although I am not yet three,
this moment is forever etched
upon my moonstruck soul,

And the music always takes me back.

Tea at Grannie's

Summer; and the cold water,
in the lemon-yellow milk bucket,
is unequal to its task,
resulting in the need
to skim creamy archipelagos
from the cups of tea.
Jelly is forsaken
in favour of canned fruit
and the butter is slick
as you spread it on the loaf,
hugged firmly to your nylon bosom,
then slice with the bread knife,
sabre-curved from sharpening,
always towards you.

We lay the table, burrowing
into the sideboard for jams;
midnight blue damson,
golden apple jelly and the spicy,
slubbed silk of rhubarb and ginger.
Back and forth to the kitchen with
plates and dishes and cutlery.
A bowl of lettuce, and celery hearts
in a Woolworth's glass; Dairylea triangles
and crimson-wrapped Cracker Barrel,
from back of the larder, under the stairs,
and ham from the butchers over the road.
Jam tarts with stalks in like tropical toadstools
and sliced slab sponge, seductive with lemon zest
beneath its brittle crust of glacé icing.
We know we've really grown up
when at last you entrust us
with carrying the brimful jug of Carnation.

Finally we sit down to feast,
bare legs slowly adhering to our chairs;
burnt umber chenille softly brushing our knees
beneath a brittle crust of starched white linen.

Soap Bubbles

First the mixing of the magic;
with a practiced hand you'd shake
a spiral of Persil into the lemon-yellow bowl,
pluck the kettle from the gas flame
and pour a steaming circle.
Then add a swirl of cold
from the rubber-nozzled tap.

Now I was allowed to stir.
Standing on the kitchen stool,
you close behind me so I couldn't fall;
my starfish hands swimming
in the milky, silky sea,
until all the sandy soap was gone
and it was time to cast the net.

Your brown hands showed the shape;
the slightly squashed oval
of thumbs and forefingers, tip to tip.
A careful dip into the opalescent mix;
then gently lift the glimmering window
and blow – a soft, silent whistle –
slowly, steadily, your breath and mine.
The soap glass would ripple, swell,
billowing, shimmered with paisley rainbows
twirling and spinning in the light;
the magic ours, for just a moment.

Bead Swapping

To the playground's chattering Kasbah
our glittering treasure trove we bring;
beads and buttons, gems and gewgaws,
in Tupperware and old tobacco tins.

Our wares, laid out on books and hankies,
sparkle in the lunch-time sun.
Baubles begged from aunts and grannies
or pirate-raided from our mums.

Silent we squat, making appraisals
with eight-year-old, swift-darting eyes;
already knowing not to be too eager
about what we'd most dearly prize.

A broken string of moon-pale pearls
buys me a tiny, brass Swiss bell;
half an hour's heated bartering
and the amethyst button is mine as well.

More than thirty years have passed
since those summer playground days,
but bell and button still have about them
a shimmer of Treasure's cachet.

Haiku

Hot air balloon floats
through evening sky; a map pin
searching for its hole.

For Sylvia at 17

Your eyes draw me
and I want to ask
what you were thinking
at that moment
when the shutter snapped
stilling you forever,
so beautifully thoughtful,
in black and white
and shades of grey.

What hopes and fears,
what secret dreams
had shaped that not-quite
smile upon your lips?
Had you been kissed?
And, if so, by whom?
And was that jacket
sky blue or scarlet?
Or maybe forest green?
Because somehow I doubt
that it was really grey.

Too late now to ask,
when I found this picture
you were already gone.
Beyond the reach
of phone or letter
and, although the blood
of yours I carry in my veins
hints at the answers,
I regret not asking;
not knowing who you were
at seventeen.

The Bird on the Fence

The day of his funeral it rains;
not a storm, or a downpour,
but soft, incessant, misty rain,
like widow's tears, from dawn,
and afterwards the bath blossoms
with the dark, curled petals
of part furled umbrellas, that weep
softly down the pipes.

Two families, neighbours, church friends,
the mourners of a gentle life,
split in factions, to drink tea
and queue along the narrow hall
for sandwiches, quiche and boiled fruitcake.
Whilst we fill the kettle, refill cups
and move between the groups;
our mourning deferred until later.

At last, everyone else is gone.
The dishes washed and put away.
The leftovers being fussed over
by a handful of cheeky sparrows,
and we four sit and talk quietly
or think, in silence, until I notice
a strange intensity upon my sister's face
and ask what she is looking at.

'The bird on the fence.'
As one, we peer beneath the net
and our eyes are met by the vivid gold,
but slightly bewildered, gaze,
of a sparrow-hawk; his slate-grey feathers
fluffed against the rain;

his yellow talons curled
bright upon the wood.

No sign now of the cheeky sparrows.
We stare at him, and he stares back,
for ten full minutes; This wasn't *quite*
what he'd expected, being Adventist.
Then he gives himself a shake
and disappears over the wet rooftops;
the soul of Man taken flight,
we wish him Godspeed,

And are comforted.

The Garden

One is nearer God's heart in a garden
where the intricacies of His designs
can be marvelled in bee wings and petals
or the twirling tendrils of a pea vine.

I envisage Him sat at His workbench
with His parchment, His pigments, His quill;
chewing the quill end whilst contemplating
whether beech leaves should be edged with a frill.

It's easy to be awed by the big things,
but, when I look at this tiny trefoil,
or a red spider mite, I'm astounded
at the work put into something so small.

The difference between annealing and tempering

When, at thirteen, I come home disillusioned
after Metalwork because Sir
has deemed my candlestick design
'Too difficult for a girl to make',
you dismiss Sir as an 'ignorant pillock',
and take down the garage key.

Under the grubby fluorescent
you shunt aside assorted heaps,
clearing a swarf-gritted space, for me,
beside you at the lathe; describing,
very clearly, chucks and tools
and what will happen if my hair gets caught.

Each week, for the rest of term,
you fill in the blanks of sexist education;
teaching me to chase and planish brass,
until I can shape a moon-cratered dish
with nothing more than ball-pein hammer,
bench and sand-filled leather bag.

You explain the difference between
annealing and tempering;
showing me how to heat copper pieces
to the right colour so I can curl
scrolled feet with vice and pliers;
ready for drilling and riveting.

I have told you Sir does not let girls
use the forge, so you instruct me in
the theory and practice of silver-soldering –
cleaning, applying flux, placing solder,
type and length of flame – with worked examples,
before checking I have everything I need.

Next day I make my preparations, wait
until Sir is busy with the boys, then set to work;
I have just finished when he finally notices –
'What d'you think you're doing?'
'Silver-soldering, Sir'
'Where on earth did you learn that?'

'My father taught me … *Sir*'

Waiting for the Glass to Fall

A treasure from a hundred years ago,
this first-floor bay of brittle, slender panes,
with tulips etched in fluid art nouveau,

Is now the very last one that remains,
unscathed by wartime bomb and rumbling bus;
defying the 'improvers' plastic frames.

But soon it will be broken shards and dust;
the shrunken, scab-skinned wood crumbles away.
Two blooms, already touched by bitter frost,

Creep closer to destruction day by day
and we'll just let a craftsman's legacy
fall victim to dispassionate decay,

So busy now, we never seem to see
how much we've lost of who we used to be.

God of Piebald Creatures

Did you have a day
when you suddenly got fed up
with having every colour of the rainbow
at your disposal?
A day when you said 'Enough
of peacocks and kingfishers;
clownfish and anemones –
let's see what I can do with pen and ink'
and took down a fresh sheet of paper?

The badger must have taken hours,
one hair black, the next white,
but such a striking face. Is that why
the skunk was so much simpler?
Was there a scribbled margin note
beside the zebra saying 'tiger – black stripes'?
Did you drop your pen, sputtering
upon the appaloosa, then drip
deliberate blots onto the orca?

Were you surprised when it took just
the faintest shading to lift the Lipizzaner's flank
and the sheerest glaze of white to turn
the panther's pelt to silken velvet?
And didn't that little practice piece
come in handy for the mole?
And wouldn't you just know the magpie
would sneak off and dip his tail in green lustre
the moment your back was turned?

Van Gogh's Bookshop

"I still have it in my heart someday to paint a bookshop with the front yellow and pink in the evening … like a light in the midst of the darkness…"

It would have been the poster
I'd have bought, in years gone by,
and Blu-tacked above my bed;
the print that would now hang,
oak framed, beside my desk
to rest my thoughts upon
when pausing between stanzas.

A place to lose myself, for just a while,
in the glory of sun-gilt stone.
The deepening cobalt of the sky
edged with duck-egg, rose and gold;
muted remnants of the sunset
swirled with the faintest shimmer
of the starry night to come.

And, glowing behind the glass,
the sumptuous striped brocade
of cloth and leather bindings
burnished by lamplight;
all woven in loving strokes of oil,
gift of the artist to renew
the fire within a poet's heart.

Haiku

Like sooty snowflakes
falling into the sunset,
crows return to roost.

Haiku Advent Calendar – 2011

Thursday 1st

Birches are sequinned;
occasionally catching
stray shafts of sunlight.

Friday 2nd

Sycamores copper –
burnished by last night's frost-fire;
roofs sparkle with rime.

Saturday 3rd

Golden afternoon
melts into crimson sunset;
shepherds delighted.

Sunday 4th

Decorated trees
appearing in windows; lights
glittering like jewels.

Monday 5th

Against ice-blue sky
bare branches of wood weave
black lace filigree.

Tuesday 6th

Paper and ribbons,
presents ready for wrapping;
happiest of chores.

Wednesday 7th

Star shining in east
alongside the moon; sudden
tingle of wonder.

Thursday 8th

Wind from the North Pole
sends fallen leaves scuttering.
Can I hear sleigh bells?

Friday 9th	Full moon peeps coyly through chiffon ribbons of clouds; shiny as sixpence.
Saturday 10th	Deep frost overnight; windscreens patterned with paisley; breath hangs in the air.
Sunday 11th	Black Cap steals scarlet cotoneaster berries; Robin keeps look out.
Monday 12th	Hanging up baubles of crimson and gold; feeling suddenly festive.
Tuesday 13th	Wind shifting to north brings clouds of arctic fox white; rain has claws of ice.
Wednesday 14th	Awoken early by cool finger of moonlight gently stroking cheek.
Thursday 15th	Sunshine after storm casts rainbows through sun-catcher; hope dances on walls.
Friday 16th	Silence of snowflakes, working their magic, wakes us to transfigured world.
Saturday 17th	Finish writing cards; post box filled with good wishes and hopes for New Year.

Sunday 18th	Great feathers falling from blue-grey quilted sky; earth longs for a blanket.
Monday 19th	Quiet evening in listening to carols and music laced with snow.
Tuesday 20th	Sunrise is pastel; a dish of sugared almonds, palest pinks and mauves.
Wednesday 21st	Letterbox rattles; cards from friends and relations bring news of past year.
Thursday 22nd	Solstice is golden; sun making the very best of its shortest day.
Friday 23rd	Last minute wrapping, exchanging hugs and kisses, gifts all delivered.
Saturday 24th	Single voice sings 'Once In Royal David's City'; Christmas almost here.
Midnight	The cry of a Child within a starlit stable sends echoes through time.

The Christmas Poems

2004 – Christmas Wishes

Wishing you the magic of Christmas
that sparkles in snowflakes and stars;
that glows in the eyes of small children
and nestles in all of our hearts.

May your Christmas be happy and joyful,
scented with spices and pine;
bauble'd with laughter and carols,
and memories to last for all time.

2005 – Something to Hang on Your Tree

Choosing pieces from my workbox,
I add a skein of silk
the colour of holly berries, and delve
amongst the beads and sequins
for just the right green glass leaves,
a pinch of golden stars
and a single, perfect snowflake.

Now I can sew.
Setting each stitch with care;
each star one of wonder,
each leaf a hint of Christmas spice,
laced with the Season's crimson joy
and the sparkle of snow magic,
to create this little heart
for your Christmas tree
from me, to you, with love.

2006 – Snow Witch

"Snow Witch, Snow Witch
tell me, what do you make?"
"I'm weaving a blanket
for the world, lest it wake.

With spun strands of stardust
I have threaded my loom.
The shuttle I've loaded
with pearl-sheen of the moon.

The wild geese have given
cloud-white down from their breasts
before they flew away
to their wintering rests.

From the wastes of the north
comes a hank of ice chills,
that I can twist with a
sparkling spool full of thrills.

The essence of mountains,
the sharp scent of green pines,
the taste of enchantment,
all shall be intertwined.

A spell for protection
and a charm for rebirth;
my blanket will ensure
Spring sleeps safe in the Earth."

2007 – The Shepherd's Tale

We'd lit a fire that night on the hillside,
the weather had turned cold from mild,
when sudden, from far, on the cobalt air,
came the midnight cry of a child.

The Earth, it trembled beneath us,
and the stars seemed to dance in the skies.
A glorious light shone all around
and, for a moment, blinded our eyes.

Then there by the fire stood an angel,
with great wings, and in gold arrayed,
and a face of such beauty it smote us
and we dropped to our knees, sore afraid.

But he bade us 'Fear Not' and told us
great joy had come to us and all men,
and he spoke of a Saviour born to us,
in a stable, down in Bethlehem.

A whole choir of angels appeared then,
singing above in the starlit sky
of peace and goodwill upon Earth,
and glory to God upon high.

We stood on the hillside in wonder
at the new star shining over our heads
and knew that we had to follow it
and see to what treasure it led.

It stopped over a rough wooden stable,
back behind the Old Camel Inn;
we stood at the doorway and listened
and heard the murmur of voices within.

We stepped in over the threshold
and there in the manger He lay;
a new babe wrapped in swaddling bands
in a nest of summer-sweet hay.

We told them the angel had sent us
and the young Mother quietly smiled
whilst we knelt in the hay and worshiped
Her seemingly slumbering Child.

When we looked up, His eyes were wide open
and the pure, clear love in His gaze
blazed right down to the depths of our souls
and has burned there all of our days.

2008 – Stockings

I've had many Christmas stockings,
but the very best of all
were Dad's brown, woolly, wellie socks
we used when we were small.

We'd peg them on the dresser drawers
before bed on Christmas Eve
and Christmas morning they'd be stuffed
as full as they could be.

We'd delve into their lumpiness,
bring out puzzles, books and toys;
marvelling just how Santa knew
the things we'd most enjoy.

And in amongst the things to keep
Christmas treats he'd thought we'd like;
fondant ladybirds, candy canes,
string-tailed pink sugar mice,

And down at the very bottom,
as far as our arms would go,
a bag of chocolate coins
and a Satsuma in the toe.

Dad's old brown, woolly, wellie socks
have long since been thrown away
but, sometimes, my hand-stitched stocking
is full on Christmas Day.

There could be some theatre tickets,
a new novel to enjoy;
marzipan fruits and purple gloves,
I guess they're 'grown-up' toys.

But a Christmas stocking has to have
(however 'up' I grow)
a bag of chocolate coins
and a Satsuma in the toe.

2009 – Decorating the Tree

A
star at
the
top
shining
so bright,
baubles and
tinsel reflecting
the lights.
Fragrance of
cinnamon and the
sharp scent of fir, calling to
mind sweet incense and myrrh.
Gingerbread reindeer
and striped candy canes; mini
felt stockings and red paper chains.
Once all the old treasures
have been unwrapped and hung,
we know that Christmas has truly begun;
our tree's full of magic and sparkles like snow
with
beribboned
packages
piled up
below.

2010 – Nursery Rhyme for the 21st Century

Christmas is coming,
all the shops are packed,
will you spare a pound
for the Big Issue seller's hat?

If you haven't got a pound
50p will do;
it's five below zero
and his fingertips are blue.

He doesn't speak much English,
but he has the widest smile;
even though he's desperately worried
how he'll feed his wife and child.

If usually you pass him by,
today, just pause and think,
of the reason why you're buying
presents, food and drink.

And remember that in Bethlehem,
two thousand years ago,
all this started with a family
who had nowhere left to go.

2011 – Do you believe?

Do you still wait,
breath bated,
for the strike
of midnight
Christmas Eve?
Do you believe?

Do you dream of snow;
of walking home
as the brightest star
begins to shine
in the East?
Do you believe?

Do you awaken wondering
if you just heard
the faintest ring
of silver sleigh bells
from your eaves?
Do you believe?

Do the gifts you give,
however big, or small,
whoever for,
bring you more joy
than those received?
Do you believe?

Does the scent of pine,
cinnamon, mulled wine;
the glow of firelight,
the sparking tree
still conjure magic?
Do you believe?

I wait with bated breath,
I dream of snow,
I hear the bells,
I love to give,
and I believe
the magic lives.

2012 – Christmas Countdown

His alarm clock goes off early;
he's got lots to do today
and he's soon down in the stables
filling mangers up with hay.

The last few lists are coming in;
so, when the reindeer are all groomed,
he picks out the final presents
and heads for the Wrapping Room.

Once every gift is wrapped and tagged
and every list stamped 'Done',
he stops for a quick sandwich,
hot chocolate and a bun.

He takes the bulging sacks outside
and loads the sleigh again;
not forgetting the Satsuma's,
chocolate coins and candy canes.

He leads the reindeer out in pairs
and puts their harness on.
(Yesterday he oiled the leather
and polished the bells until they shone.)

He feeds the cat and banks the fire,
and turns the lamp down low.
Then puts on his scarlet coat and hat;
it's time for him to go.

A last check to make sure the parcels
are safely stowed inside the sleigh.
He shakes the reins, the bells ring out
and Santa's on his way!

Indigo Dreams Publishing
132, Hinckley Road
Stoney Stanton
Leicestershire
LE9 4LN
www.indigodreams.co.uk